HAWAII

in words and pictures

BY DENNIS B. FRADIN

MAPS BY LEN W. MEENTS

Consultant:
Elizabeth P. Dunford
Hawaiiana Author

 CHILDRENS PRESS, CHICAGO

Hawaiian sunset, Oahu

Library of Congress Cataloging in Publication Data
Fradin, Dennis B.
    Hawaii in words and pictures.

    SUMMARY: A brief history of the Aloha State with
a description of its countryside and major cities.
    1. Hawaii—Juvenile literature. [1. Hawaii]
I. Wahl, Richard, 1939-1 II. Meents, Len W.
III. Title.
DU623.2.F73   996.9   79-25605
ISBN 0-516-03913-X

Picture Acknowledgments:
HAWAII VISITORS BUREAU—Cover, pages 5, 12, 26, 27 (left), 31 (right),
32, 33, 34, 36, 37 (left)
MICHAEL S. PICKARD—pages 2, 15 (right), 17 (left and top), 29, 30
SHELDON MILLMAN—pages 6, 7, 8, 14, 15 (left), 21, 23, 25, 31 (left), 35,
37 (right), 38, 39
ERWIN S. PICKARD—pages 10, 17 (bottom), 27 (right)
KAHUKU SUGAR MILL—page 18
CHANDLER FORMAN—page 40
COVER—Volcanoes National Park

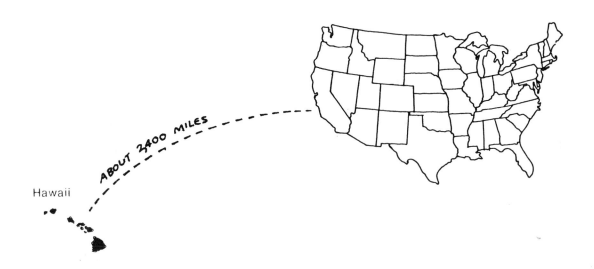

The name *Hawaii* (hah • WYE • ee) is thought to come from a man named *Hawaii-loa* (hah • WYE • ee-LOH • ah). He may have led the first people to Hawaii in canoes. Hawaii may also refer to *Hawaiki* (hah • WYE • kee). This was said to be the distant land from where the people sailed.

Hawaii is the only state that is not part of the mainland of North America. It is a group of islands in the Pacific Ocean. Hawaii is one of our loveliest states. It has warm, sandy beaches. It has blue ocean waters. Trees and flowers fill the state with bright colors and sweet smells. Waterfalls plunge down the sides of green mountains.

Do you know which is the leading pineapple-growing area in the world?

Do you know where the world's biggest volcano lies?

Do you know where enemy planes once bombed United States soil at a place called Pearl Harbor?

Do you know which is the *newest* state?

As you will learn, the answer to all these questions is: Hawaii.

Millions of years ago there was no land of Hawaii. There was only the Pacific Ocean. A big crack opened on the ocean floor. Hot liquid rock—called *lava* (LAH • vah)—poured out of this crack. Lava piled up higher and higher. It cooled. It formed underwater mountains. They were called *volcanoes*.

More and more lava burst through the volcanoes. They grew higher and higher. One day their tops poked above the ocean waters. These mountaintops became the Hawaiian Islands. The islands to the northwest were formed first. They are the oldest. The island of Hawaii is

Lava fountain in Kilauea Crater at Hawaii Volcanoes National Park

farthest to the east. It is the newest of the Hawaiian island chain. Volcanoes on that island still erupt. Lava still pours out. That island is still being formed.

Over more millions of years, some of the rocky lava crumbled. It became soil. Waves and rain wore down the islands. Birds flew to the islands. They carried seeds. The seeds were dropped on Hawaii. They took root in the rich soil. A few seeds were carried by ocean waters. Some were blown by the wind. Rain helped the seeds grow into the green plants that cover Hawaii today.

Scientists say this is the way the Hawaiian Islands were formed. But early Hawaiians told another story. They said that the god Maui (MAUW • ee) dropped fishhooks into the ocean. Instead of fish, he caught Hawaii. He pulled the islands up from the ocean floor. He liked what he saw. He didn't throw them back.

How did the first people get to the Hawaiian Islands?

It is thought that, long ago, people sailed from Asia. These people are known as *Polynesians* (pahl • ih • NEE • zhunz). They traveled in huge canoes. The canoes may have been 100 feet long. The Polynesians settled on islands in the Pacific Ocean. From these islands, some Polynesians sailed northward. They traveled for thousands of miles. To survive, they carried food. They

Early Polynesians traveled to Hawaii in canoes like this one, only much larger.

Early Hawaiians built houses of branches and grass. This one, built much later, is at Polynesian Cultural Center on Oahu.

ate fish caught in the ocean. Only the stars told them which way they were going. "Will we find land—or will we keep going forever?" the people must have wondered. Finally, they sighted the islands of Hawaii. They settled there. These first Hawaiians arrived on the islands about 2,000 years ago. Another group came to Hawaii from Tahiti (tah • HEE • tee) about 800 years ago.

These early Hawaiians built houses of branches and grass. Many houses made a village. They had brought animals and seeds on their huge canoes. They planted crops. They raised chickens and pigs. They made fishhooks and nets. They caught fish. Coconuts, sweet potatoes, bananas, fish, chickens, and pigs provided food.

During the Polynesian Cultural Center boat show you can see the kind of feather cloaks once worn by Hawaiian chiefs.

One main food was called *poi* (POY). It was made from the taro plant. First the large, underground stems were cooked. Then they were pounded into a paste. Hawaiians ate *poi* nearly every day. They ate a lot of *poi*. Many early Hawaiians weighed 300 or even 400 pounds. To them, fat was beautiful. Many early Hawaiians were very tall. Some were six and a half feet or more.

In these days long ago, each island had chiefs, or rulers. A chief could wear a helmet and cloak made of thousands of colorful bird feathers. Laws were strict. People had to give some crops to their chief. If the chief wanted more land, he could give the order to fight.

The Hawaiians had *kapus* (KAH • pooz). These were rules saying what they could not do. A person who stepped on the shadow of a high chief could be killed. Women and men were not allowed to eat together. Another *kapu* concerned fish. When fishermen prepared their hooks, they kept quiet. "Fish have ears," they said. "They will swim away if they hear us."

The people believed in many gods. There were gods in the sea, in the rocks, and in the trees. Lono was the god of the harvest. Pele (PEH • lay) was the volcano goddess. She was said to live in volcanoes. Hawaiians said that the gods might punish anyone who broke a *kapu*.

Hawaiians knew how to have fun, too. They had a four-month holiday starting in November. They had great feasts. They had many sports contests. Hawaiians made wooden surfboards. On them they rode tall waves toward shore. The chiefs had sleds. On them they slid down rock slides.

Hawaiians had a dance called the *hula* (HOO • lah). By moving their hands and bodies, the dancers told a story. Some hula dances praised gods or chiefs. Some of the stories were about long canoe voyages. Others were about the forces of nature.

These early people had no written language. How is all this known about them? Some of their buildings and tools remain. Old stories and chants have given us more clues.

Hula dances are still performed in Hawaii

For hundreds of years, the only visitors were birds. They came to spend their winters in the warm islands.

Explorers may have stopped at Hawaii in the 1500s. Then, on January 18, 1788, English Captain James Cook arrived. He came with two ships. They were the *Discovery* (dis • KUHV • er • ee) and the *Resolution* (rez • oh • LOO • shun). Cook went to these islands by accident. He wasn't looking for Hawaii. He was looking for a waterway through North America.

Captain Cook kept a log, or diary. "Natives came out in their canoes to meet us," he wrote. "They seemed very happy that we had come." The Hawaiians met the Englishmen in friendship. The harvest god Lono was said to have light skin and hair. The Hawaiians may have thought that Captain Cook was Lono. They gave Captain Cook a feather cloak. They gave food to him and to his men. Captain Cook explored the islands. He made maps.

Captain Cook and his ships left Hawaii on February 4, 1779. A storm caught the ships on the ocean. They returned to Hawaii. No one knows exactly how the friendship turned into fighting. The Hawaiians may have felt that the Englishmen had taken advantage of them. One Hawaiian stole a small boat from the *Discovery*. Foolishly, Captain Cook kidnapped a Hawaiian chief. Hawaiians and Englishmen gathered to fight near the seashore on the island of Hawaii. The Englishmen fired some shots. The Hawaiians fought with clubs and knives. Captain Cook was killed in this fight. Six Hawaiian chiefs were also killed. Captain Cook was buried in Kealakekua (kay • AH • lah • kay • KOO • ah) Bay.

Monument to Captain Cook on the island of Hawaii

Soon after, other explorers and traders arrived in the Hawaiian Islands.

Kamehameha (kah • MAY • hah • MAY • hah) was a young chief. He was a warrior. He was from the island of Hawaii. He had seen the fighting between his people and Captain Cook. Kamehameha decided that he alone would rule all the Hawaiian Islands. At that time many different chiefs ruled on the islands.

Kamehameha won over part of his home island— Hawaii. There were many battles. In one battle, many men in the army of his enemy were killed in a strange way. They were killed by an eruption of the Kilauea (keel • ow • WAY • ah) volcano. "Even the goddess Pele is on Kamehameha's side!" some people said. There were many stories about his magical powers.

View from Nuuanu Pali

Kamehameha was ruler of the whole island of Hawaii by about 1792. He then gathered a huge army. They traveled by canoe. Kamehameha took over the island of Maui. Then he took the islands of Lanai (lah • NYE) and Molokai (MOH • loh • KYE). He landed at Waikiki (WYE • kee • KEE) Beach. That is on the island of Oahu (oh • WAH • hoo). On Oahu there are cliffs. One of the cliffs is Nuuanu Pali (noo • AH • noo PAH • lee). Pali is the Hawaiian word for cliff. On Oahu, Kamehameha met an army of another king. Kamehameha and his men drove the army over Nuuanu Pali.

By 1810, Kamehameha was king of all the Hawaiian Islands. He built temples for the gods. During his rule more and more *haole* (HOW • lay) people came to Hawaii. *Haole* people are foreigners (FOR • en • erz). American whaling ships stopped in Hawaii. Hawaiians sold them supplies. American trading ships came, too. The traders bought sandalwood from the Hawaiians. They sold the wood in China. Sandalwood is a sweet-smelling wood. It was used to make fancy carved objects.

King Kamehameha saw that outsiders wanted his land. "Foreigners want my islands," he said. "This will not happen so long as I live. We must always keep the old ways," he said.

Left: Statue of King Kamehameha
Below: Ki'i (idols) may still be seen in the islands.

Kamehameha and his family ruled the islands for about the next 100 years. Changes did come. Kamehameha I died. The *kapu* system was done away with. Most Hawaiians felt that the gods and goddesses had no power. Kamehameha II even left his homeland. He went to visit England with his wife. They caught measles and died. Old Hawaiians said: "The gods are angry. They have done this." But the old ways were dying.

In 1820 American missionaries began coming to Hawaii. They wanted the Hawaiians to become Christians. The *kapu* system was gone. The old religion was gone. So most Hawaiians did become Christians. The missionaries taught the people to read and write.

In 1840 Hawaii's first constitution (con • stih • TOO • shun) was adopted. These laws protected people. Soon people were allowed to own their own land. They were allowed to keep all their crops. No chief could order people to go out and fight.

Many citizens of Hawaii are Buddhists.
They have built shrines and temples in the islands.
Above: A Buddhist shrine
Left: A Buddhist temple
Far left: A pagoda-style temple

More foreigners came to the islands. They came from the United States, China, Japan, the Philippines (FILL • ih • peenz), England, and many other places. Most of them came to work on the sugar plantations. Many married Hawaiians. They had families. Schools, churches, stores, and other buildings were built. There were fewer and fewer native Hawaiians. At one time there were as many as 300,000 of them. Diseases brought by the foreigners killed many Hawaiians. Today only about 1 percent of the population is pure Hawaiian.

The Kuhuku Sugar Mill, on the North Shore of Oahu, has been restored.

In the 1850s sugar-growing became big business in Hawaii. Much of the sugar crop was sent to the United States. There it was used to sweeten foods. Pineapple growing also became a big business.

Liliuokalani (lee • lee • yoh • kah • LAH • nee) became queen in 1891. Powerful American sugar-growers did not like the queen's laws. They wanted Hawaii to become part of the United States. In 1893, Liliuokalani was removed from the throne. This was the end of royal rule in Hawaii. American businessmen were in control.

Today, Queen Liliuokalani is known for writing the famous song "Aloha Oe" (ah • LO • ha OY). It means "Farewell to Thee." She might have been saying goodbye to a way of life. Many Hawaiian customs lived on. But many of the old ways were gone.

In 1898 Hawaii became a part of the United States. In 1900 it became the Territory of Hawaii. It wasn't a state yet. The people were American citizens. But they couldn't vote for the president. They didn't have all the rights that people in the states had. Sanford B. Dole was the son of a missionary. He was made the first governor of the territory. Governors of Hawaii were appointed by the president of the United States.

Hawaii lies in the middle of the Pacific Ocean. The United States knew that Hawaii could be a good stopping-place for their navy ships. In the early 1900s the United States Navy built a big base at Pearl Harbor, in Honolulu (hoh • noh • LOO • loo). This became an important navy base for United States ships.

Hawaii was sending sugar to the United States. It was sending pineapples. And now it was a navy base. "Hawaii should be a state," said many people. They felt that the United States was using Hawaii. They felt that the Hawaiian people were not getting much in return. Starting in 1903, many people worked to make the Hawaiian Islands a state. But the United States Congress wouldn't vote to make Hawaii a state. "The people of Hawaii won't support the United States in case of war," said some lawmakers. Something happened to prove them wrong.

December 7, 1941 was a lovely Sunday morning. A fleet of United States ships sat in Pearl Harbor. Airplanes stood at Hickam Field. Much of the world was at war. It was not known whether the United States would enter the war. Suddenly, at 7:55 A.M., Japanese planes swooped down on Pearl Harbor. They dropped bombs for two hours. About 170 planes were destroyed. Many ships were sunk. More than 2,400 people were

The National Memorial Cemetery of the Pacific
in Punchbowl Crater honors the dead of World War II.

killed. President Franklin Delano Roosevelt made a
speech. He called the December 7 attack on Pearl
Harbor "a date which will live in infamy." The United
States now entered World War II (1939-1945).

Hawaiian people fought hard for the United States.
Many of them had Japanese backgrounds. This helped
convince the United States Congress that Hawaii
deserved to be a state. In March of 1959 the United
States Congress approved statehood for Hawaii.
President Eisenhower signed the statehood bill. Most
Hawaiians voted for statehood.

On August 21, 1959, Hawaii became the fiftieth state. Hawaiians set off fireworks. Newspaper headlines read "STATEHOOD!" Honolulu was the biggest city in Hawaii. It was the capital. "Hawaii Ponoi" (poh • NOY) was the Hawaii national anthem. It means "Hawaii's Own." It was made the state song. The words to this song had been written by King Kalakaua (kah • lah • KOW • ah). He wrote the song long before Hawaiians dreamed of statehood. *Aloha* is a Hawaiian word meaning "love." It is the way Hawaiians say hello to people. It is also the way they say good-bye. Hawaii was nicknamed the *Aloha State.* The Aloha State is the newest of the 50 states.

Today, people from the United States mainland flock to Hawaii. Most of them go in the winter. The warm weather and scenery make Hawaii a leading tourist state.

All these tourists need places to stay. Hotels and resorts have been built on the islands of Oahu, Hawaii,

View of Honolulu and Diamond Head

Kauai, Molokai, and Maui. This angers many people. Beautiful beaches and scenery are being destroyed. There have been some successful fights to preserve the island paradise. But more tourists come. More buildings keep going up.

Sometimes, Mother Nature reminds Hawaiians of how their islands came to be. In 1950 the volcano Mauna Loa (MAUW • nah LOH • ah) erupted. It produced one of the biggest lava flows of modern times. In 1960 the city of Hilo (HEE • loh) was hit by a huge tidal wave. It killed 61 people. In 1975, when Kilauea erupted, huge earthquakes shook the island of Hawaii.

23

You have learned about some of Hawaii's history. Now it is time for a trip—in words and pictures—through the Aloha State.

How beautiful this state looks from the air! There are 132 islands in the Hawaiian Island chain. They are strung out like green gems against the blue Pacific Ocean. Most of these islands are small. There are no people on them. There are eight main islands.

They are: Hawaii (hah • WYE • ee)

Maui (MAUW • ee)

Molokai (MOH • loh • KYE)

Kahoolawe (KAH • ho • LAH • vay)

Lanai (lah • NYE)

Oahu (oh • WAH • hoo)

Kauai (kah • WAH • ee)

Niihau (NEE • how)

Your airplane is over the island of Oahu. "Oahu" means the *Gathering Place.* Most of the state's people— about 80 percent—live on this one island. Honolulu is on

Oahu. It is the state's biggest city. Honolulu is also the capital of the state.

You have landed at Honolulu International Airport. When you arrive in Honolulu, a *lei* (LAY) may be placed around your neck. A *lei* is a flower necklace. Hawaiians greet you with *"Aloha!"*

Long ago, Hawaiians built a village where the city of Honolulu now stands. In 1794 English Captain William Brown sailed into Honolulu Harbor. Later, whaling and other ships went in and out of the harbor. Visit the Pearl Harbor Naval Base. It was attacked on the "day of infamy" during World War II. A ship, the U.S.S. *Arizona,* still lies under the water.

The U.S.S. *Arizona* Memorial at Pearl Harbor

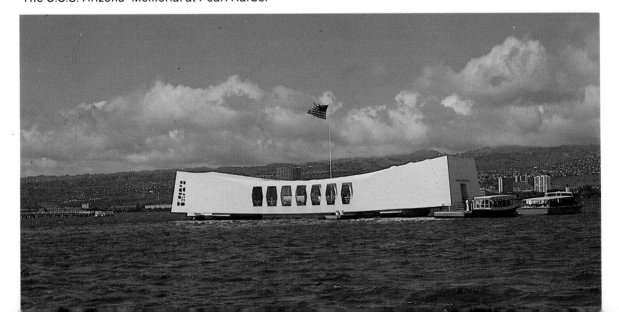

The state capitol building in Honolulu

Visit the state capitol building in Honolulu. This is where men and women meet to make laws for the Aloha State.

The Iolani (ee • oh • LAH • nee) Palace is across the street from the capitol building. King Kalakaua and Queen Liliuokalani once lived there.

Go to the top of the tall Aloha Tower. From there you can see that Honolulu is a modern city.

Don't stay indoors too long in Honolulu. The city has beautiful beaches, mountains, and gardens. Diamond Head is an extinct volcano. That means it is no longer active. It doesn't erupt.

Nearby is Waikiki Beach, where people swim and surf. Diamond Head and Waikiki Beach are two of the most famous places in the state.

Luau (LOO • ow) feasts of Hawaiian food are held at Waikiki. Roast pig and many other dishes are served. Singers and hula dancers entertain.

There are other lovely places on the island of Oahu. Visit Nuuanu Pali, near Honolulu. From this steep cliff you can get a breathtaking view of the island. It wasn't beautiful to a group of warriors long ago. Kamehameha's army forced many enemy warriors over this cliff in 1795.

On Waikiki Beach, with Diamond Head in the background, people swim, surf, sunbathe, and build sand castles.

Visit the Polynesian Cultural Center. There you can see six different kinds of Polynesian villages.

Surfing was a sport in Hawaii hundreds of years ago. Every December, the International Surfing Championships are held at Makaha (mah • KAH • hah) Beach on Oahu. People stand on boards and ride huge waves toward shore. You may wonder how people can surf in December. It is bitter cold in much of the United States. The Aloha State is warm in December—often about 75°F. The state has temperatures in the 70s and 80s most of the time.

You'll have to take a plane or a boat to the other islands of the state. The biggest island in the state of Hawaii is the island of Hawaii. It is nicknamed the *Big Island*. It is about twice as big as all the other islands in the state put together.

A lava field on the island of Hawaii

This island was formed by five big volcanoes. Two of these volcanoes (Mauna Loa and Kilauea) are still active. That means they still sometimes erupt. You can see these two volcanoes at Hawaii Volcanoes National Park.

Mauna Loa means "long mountain." It is the biggest volcano in the world. Lava from Mauna Loa has flowed down to the ocean. In 1926, lava from Mauna Loa swept away a whole fishing village. Once, the Air Force had to drop bombs on a lava flow. That kept it from hitting the city of Hilo.

Kilauea is on one of Mauna Loa's slopes. A highway passes near Kilauea Crater. Kilauea is called a "drive-in volcano" because people can get so close to it. From the highway they can watch the bubbling lava and the fires in the crater. Sometimes there is a big eruption. When that happens everyone gets out of the way. The lava is boiling. Some people watch eruptions from airplanes. In 1955 there was a big eruption. And in 1959 one of Kilauea's craters sent lava nearly 2,000 feet into the air.

There is black sand on the island of Hawaii. You can see it at the Kaimu (KYE • moo) Black Sand Beach. The sand is made of grains of lava.

Kaimu Black Sand Beach

A cowboy *(paniolo)* on the Parker Ranch

Much sugar cane is grown on the island. Coffee is grown, too. And so are tasty macadamia (mack • ah • DAY • mee • ah) nuts. They are often used in cakes and ice cream. The Parker Ranch on the island is one of the biggest cattle ranches in the United States. It was started by an American sailor. His name was John Parker. The cowboys on this ranch sing Hawaiian songs. They play ukuleles (oo • koo • LAY • layz).

Hilo is the biggest city on this island. It is a port city. Sugar, coffee, nuts, and other products are shipped by boat from Hilo.

Rainbow
Falls Park

Near Hilo there are some beautiful sights. Akaka (ah •
KAH • kah) Falls plunges 424 feet over a cliff on a
volcanic mountain. Another waterfall, Rainbow Falls, is
also near Hilo.

The island of Maui is called the *Valley Island.* It was
named for the god Maui. He was said to have captured
the sun. He only let it go when the sun promised to slow
down. This would give Hawaiians more hours for
working. Today, there is an observatory (ub • ZUR • vuh •
tore • ee) on Maui. There scientists study the sun and the
stars.

Mount Haleakala (hah • LAY • ah • KAH • lah) is on Maui. It is an inactive volcano. From the top sides of the crater, you can sometimes see your shadow on the clouds. This is called the "Specter of the Brocken."

Lovely Waianapanapa (wye • AH • nah • pah • NAH • pah) Cave is on this island. According to legend, this underwater cave was the meeting-place of lovers of long ago.

Left: Iao Valley on Maui. In the background is the Iao Needle.
Below: Haleakala Crater, Maui.

Shipwreck Beach, Lanai

Cake, ice cream, and soft drinks are made with sugar. You can go for miles on Maui and see nothing but fields of sugar cane. The sugar comes from the juice in the stalk of the sugar cane plant. Sugar cane needs a warm climate. It needs plenty of water. The state of Hawaii is perfect for sugar cane.

Kahului (kah • hoo • LOO • ee) is the island's biggest city. From there sugar and pineapples are sent out on ships.

On the island of Lanai pineapple is king. Lanai is called the *Pineapple Island.* It is owned by a pineapple company. No other state—or country—grows as much pineapple as Hawaii. And most of it is grown on Lanai.

A young pineapple plant looks something like a pine cone.

You can see how pineapples are grown on the island. Miles of green pineapple plants are planted. The pineapples take nearly two years to grow. Machines can pick 25,000 ripe pineapples in an hour. Then the pineapples go to the cannery. Some pineapples are squeezed for juice. Others are sliced and canned. They are shipped from Lanai to places around the world.

Molokai is nicknamed the *Friendly Island*. Pineapples are grown there, too. There are cattle ranches on Molokai. And deer live in the island's forests.

There is a statue of a priest on Molokai. His name was Father Damien de Veuster (DAY • mee • uhn deh • VYOU • ster). In years past, people with leprosy (Hansen's disease) were sent away from their homes. Many were sent to Molokai. They went to an out-of-the-way part of the island. There they spent the rest of their lives.

Father Damien was sent to Molokai as a priest for these people. He had to serve as a doctor as well. Father Damien caught leprosy. He died of it in 1889. Today, the disease can be treated with drugs. At the Kalaupapa (kah • lauw • PAH • pah) Leper Colony, you can see where Father Damien lived and worked.

The Friendly Island is also famous for having more native Hawaiians than any other place in the world.

Mule trail, Molokai, with Kalaupapa in the background

Kahoolawe is one Hawaiian island you *can't* visit. This small island is nicknamed *Target Island* or the *Island of Death.* Its population is zero. This is not as mysterious as it sounds. The island is used for target practice by the United States Air Force, Navy, and Army.

Kauai is nicknamed the *Garden Island.* It is very beautiful. It has lush green forests. It has many kinds of beautiful flowers. The colors are brighter than a new pack of crayons. Kauai is thought to mean the "land of plenty." The name fits.

Left: Fern Grotto, Kauai
Below: Kauai Valley farmland

Waimea Canyon, on Kauai, is called the Grand Canyon of Hawaii.

Kauai is the oldest of the islands. Mount Waialeale (wye • AH • lay • AH • lay) is near the middle of the island. It is thought to be the oldest mountain in the state. It is also one of the rainiest places in the world. One year, over 600 inches of rain fell on this mountain.

Another interesting mountain is called the Sleeping Giant. That is what the top of the mountain looks like.

Waimea (wye • MAY • ah) Canyon is on the Garden Island. Rivers and rain have carved out the canyon. The rocks on the canyon walls are red, blue, and green.

Hawaiians used to say that the first people on the islands were *menehune* (men • eh • HOO • nay). These people were said to be only three feet tall. According to stories, these little people built the Menehune Fish Pond in one day. You can still see the walls of this fish pond near Lihue (lee • HOO • way). The *menehune* were also said to have built the Menehune Ditch. This was used to bring water to their taro patches. We now believe that these were built by full-sized people. They were probably built many hundreds of years ago.

At Waimea Bay you can see Captain Cook's Landing. This is the place where Captain Cook first walked onto Hawaiian soil.

Waimea Bay

Niihau is called the *Forbidden Island*. This island is privately owned. No one can go there without an invitation from the owners. More than 200 pure Hawaiians live on Niihau. They speak the ancient Hawaiian language used long ago. Most of them work at ranching. They have no television, telephones, or cars.

Niihau did have one uninvited guest. During World War II a Japanese pilot crash landed there. The enemy pilot's papers were taken. The Hawaiians wouldn't give them back. The pilot took out his gun. He shot one Hawaiian three times. The wounded Hawaiian picked the Japanese man up. He threw him against a stone wall. Now there is a famous saying: "Never shoot a Hawaiian more than twice. The third time he gets angry."

Pupu o Niihau, rare shells found only on the island of Niihau, are used to make beautiful necklaces.

Hawaiians give their friends *leis* to say good-bye as well as hello. After you've finished your trip through the islands, drop a *lei* in the ocean. If your *lei* is washed back to land, you will one day return to the islands. Or so they say.

Islands made millions of years ago by volcanoes.

Landing place for Polynesian canoes about 2,000 years ago.

Home to King Kamehameha . . . Queen Liliuokalani . . . and Father Damien.

A state where sugar cane . . . pineapples . . . and coconuts are grown.

Land of flower-filled valleys . . . sparkling waterfalls . . . surfing . . . *luaus*.

The modern city of Honolulu . . . the island of Niihau where people follow the old ways.

This is Hawaii—the Aloha State.

Hawaiian Pronunciations

The pronunciations in this book show the way Hawaiian words sound in normal conversation. The words are usually spoken fairly rapidly. When spoken rapidly, some sounds run together. In slow speech, each syllable is sounded. Below is a list of some of the Hawaiian words used in this book. The middle column shows the conversational pronunciation. The right-hand column shows the pronunciation in very slow speech.

Aloha Oe	ah • LOH • ha OY	ah • LOH • ha OH • ee
haole	HOW • lay	HAH • oh • lay
Hawaii	hah • WYE • ee	hah • WAH • ee • ee
Hawaii-loa	hah • WYE • ee-LOH • ah	hah • WAH • ee • ee-LOH • ah
Hawaiki	hah • WYE • kee	hah • WAH • ee • kee
Kahoolawe	kah • ho • LAH • vay	kah • ho • oh • LAH • vay
Kaimu	KYE • moo	KAH • ee • moo
Kalakaua	kah • lah • KOW • ah	kah • lah • KAH • oo • ah
Kalaupapa	kah • lauw • PAH • pah	kah • lah • oo • PAH • pah
Kilauea	keel • ow • WAY • ah	keel • ah • oo • WAY • ah
Lanai	lah • NYE	lah • NAH • ee
lei	LAY	LAY • ee
Liliuokalani	lee • lee • yoh • kah • LAH • nee	lee • lee • oo • oh • kah • LAH • nee
Maui	MAUW • ee	MAH • oo • ee
Mauna Loa	MAUW • nah LOH • ah	MAH • oo • nah LOH • ah
Molokai	MOH • loh • KYE	MOH • loh • KAH • ee
muumuu	MOO • moo	MOO • oo • moo • oo
Niihau	NEE • how	NEE • ee • HAH • oo
Nuuanu Pali	noo • AH • noo PAH • lee	noo • oo • AH • noo PAH • lee
poi	POY	POH • ee
Ponoi	poh • NOY	poh • NOH • ee
Waialeale	wye • AH • lay • AH • lay	wah • ee • AH • lay • AH • lay
Waianapanapa	wye • AH • nah • pah • NAH • pah	wah • ee • AH • nah • pah • NAH • pah
Waikiki	WYE • kee • KEE	WAH • ee • kee • KEE
Waimea	wye • MAY • ah	wah • ee • MAY • ah

Facts About HAWAII

Area—6,450 square miles (47th biggest state)
Length of Island Chain Southeast to Northwest—1,523 miles
Number of Islands—132
Eight Main Islands—Hawaii, Maui, Oahu, Kauai, Molokai, Lanai, Niihau, Kahoolawe
Highest Point—13,796 feet above sea level (Mauna Kea)
Lowest Point—Sea level (along the shores of the Pacific Ocean)

Hottest Recorded Temperature—100°F. (at Pahala on Hawaii Island, on April 27, 1931)

Coldest Recorded Temperature—Minus 14°F. (at Haleakala Crater, on Maui, on January 2, 1961)

Statehood—Our 50th state, on August 21, 1959

Origin of Name Hawaii—Possibly named for Hawaii-loa, who may have led Polynesians on the first voyage to the islands; the name may also come from Hawaiki, said to be the original home of the Polynesians to the west

Capital—Honolulu

Counties—5

U.S. Senators—2

U.S. Representatives—2

State Senators—25

State Representatives—51

State Song—"Hawaii Ponoi" (words written by King Kalakaua, music by Henri Berger)

State Motto—*Ua mau ke ea o ka aina i ka pono* (Hawaiian for "The life of the land is perpetuated in righteousness," spoken by King Kamehameha III in 1843)

Nickname—Aloha State

State Flag—Adopted in 1959

State Seal—Adopted in 1959

State Tree—Kukui

State Flower—Hibiscus

State Bird—Nene (Hawaiian Goose)

Some Waterfalls—Akaka Falls, Hanapepe Falls, Waipahee Falls, Wailua Falls, Sacred Falls, Moaula Falls

Active Volcanoes—Mauna Loa (world's biggest), Kilauea Crater

Animals—Deer, pronghorn antelopes, wild goats, wild boars, mouflon (wild sheep)

Birds—Many kinds, including nene, Manchurian thrushes, quails, turkeys, partridges, albatrosses, myna birds, sparrows, cardinals, doves, owls, herons

Fishing—Tuna, marlin, swordfish, dorado

Farm Products—Sugar cane, pineapples, beef cattle, milk, coffee, bananas, avocados, papayas, hogs, poultry, macadamia nuts

Mining—Stone, sand

Manufacturing—Canned and packaged food products, stone products, glass products, clothes, furniture

Population—769,913 (1970 census; 40th most populous state)
           865,000 (1975 estimated population)

Population Distribution—83 percent urban
                        17 percent rural

Population Density—119 people per square mile

Major Cities—Honolulu 335,000 (1975 estimates)
           Kailua 37,500
           Kaneohe 33,500
           Hilo 29,000
           Waipahu 27,200
           Pearl City 22,200

Hawaii History

About 2,000 years ago the first people (Polynesians) arrived in huge canoes from other islands in the Pacific ocean.

1200s—People arrive from Tahiti

1758—King Kamehameha I is born about this year

1778—English Captain James Cook explores Hawaiian Islands

1779—Englishmen and Hawaiians battle; Captain Cook, six Hawaiian chiefs, and others are killed

1789—The first American ship, the *Eleanore,* reaches Hawaii

1792-1795—King Kamehameha I and his army fight and conquer all islands except for Niihau and Kauai

1797—King Kamehameha I creates "Law of the Splintered Paddle" to protect travelers

1810—Kamehameha now rules all of the Hawaiian Islands

1819—Kamehameha I dies; the *kapu* system is ended by his son, Kamehameha II

1820—First missionaries arrive from United States, converting Hawaiians to Christianity

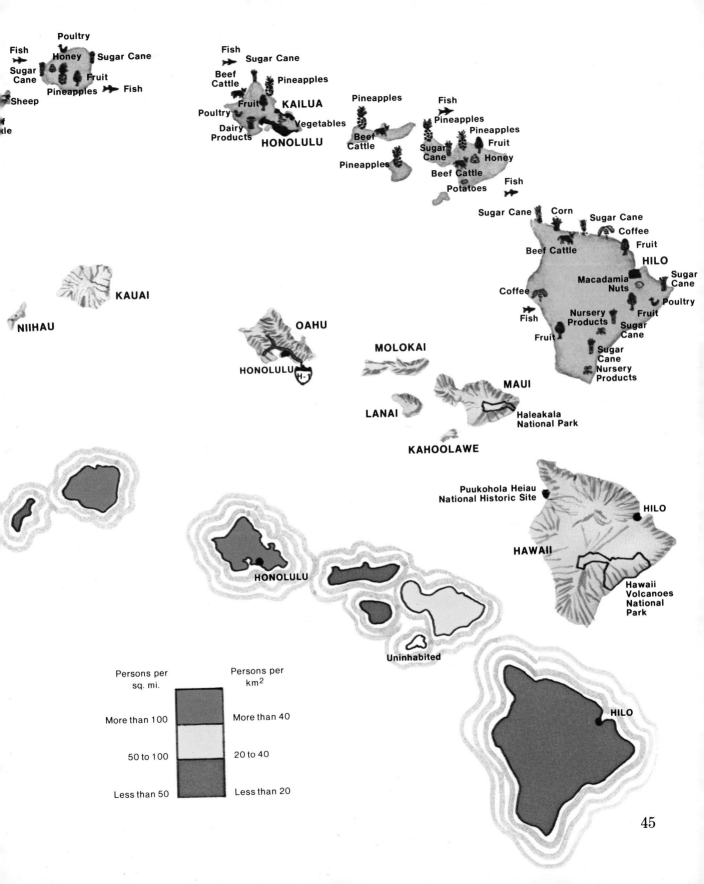

Fish
Poultry
Honey
Sugar Cane
Sugar Cane
Fruit
Pineapples
Fish
Sheep

Fish
Sugar Cane
Beef Cattle
Pineapples
Fruit
KAILUA
Poultry
Vegetables
Dairy Products
HONOLULU

Pineapples
Beef Cattle
Pineapples

Fish
Pineapples
Pineapples
Pineapples
Fruit
Sugar Cane
Honey
Beef Cattle
Fish
Potatoes

Sugar Cane
Corn
Sugar Cane
Coffee
Fruit
Beef Cattle
HILO
Coffee
Macadamia Nuts
Sugar Cane
Fish
Nursery Products
Fruit
Poultry
Fruit
Sugar Cane
Fruit
Sugar Cane
Nursery Products

KAUAI

NIIHAU

OAHU

MOLOKAI

HONOLULU
H-1

LANAI

MAUI
Haleakala National Park

KAHOOLAWE

Puukohola Heiau
National Historic Site
HILO

HONOLULU

HAWAII

Hawaii Volcanoes National Park

Uninhabited

HILO

Persons per sq. mi.	Persons per km²
More than 100	More than 40
50 to 100	20 to 40
Less than 50	Less than 20

45

1825—First coffee and sugar plantations are established about this time

1840—The Kingdom of Hawaii has its first written constitution

1840s—The United States, Great Britain, and France recognize Kingdom of Hawaii

1852—Flow of Chinese people to Hawaii, where many work in sugar cane fields

1859—First gas lights in Hawaii

1874—King Kalakaua, the "Merry Monarch," begins rule; he restores many customs banned by missionaries

1878—First telephones in Hawaii

1883—Iolani Palace is built

1885—About this time the pineapple industry begins in Hawaii

1887—United States is given right to use Pearl Harbor as navy base

1893—Queen Liliuokalani is removed from throne in "bloodless revolution"; end of rule of kings and queens in Hawaii

1894—Republic of Hawaii is established with Sanford B. Dole as president

1898—Hawaii becomes part of United States

1900—Territory of Hawaii is established on June 14

1901—Hawaiian Pineapple Company is organized by James Dole, cousin of Sanford Dole

1903—Hawaii lawmakers first ask for statehood

1919—Mauna Loa and Kilauea volcanoes have big eruptions

1919—First bill for Hawaiian statehood introduced to U.S. Congress

1926—Lava from Mauna Loa destroys a fishing village

1927—First airplane flight from mainland United States to Hawaii is made by Army lieutenants A.F. Hegenberger and L.J. Maitland

1934—Franklin Delano Roosevelt is first U.S. President to visit Hawaii

1936—Beginning of regular airplane transportation between Hawaii and mainland

1941—On December 7, 1941, Japanese attack Pearl Harbor; United States enters World War II

1941-1945—During World War II, thousands of people from Hawaii fight for United States

1950—Mauna Loa produces biggest lava flow in modern history

1957—First telephone cable from United States mainland to Hawaii

1959—Hawaii becomes the 50th state on August 21!

1962—Terminal for jet airplanes is finished at Honolulu International Airport; tourist industry is becoming bigger and bigger

1968—Present state constitution is adopted

1969—State Capitol building is completed in Honolulu

1970—Population of Aloha State is 769,913

1975—Two huge earthquakes and a tidal wave hit Island of Hawaii

1976—In Bicentennial year, over 3 million tourists visit Aloha State

1978—George R. Ariyoshi is elected to second term as governor

1979—Happy 20th birthday, Aloha State!

INDEX

47

About the Author:

Dennis Fradin attended Northwestern University on a creative writing scholarship and graduated in 1967. While still at Northwestern, he published his first stories in *Ingenue* magazine and also won a prize in *Seventeen's* short story competition. A prolific writer, Dennis Fradin has been regularly publishing stories in such diverse places as *The Saturday Evening Post, Scholastic, National Humane Review, Midwest,* and *The Teaching Paper.* He has also scripted several educational films. Since 1970 he has taught second grade reading in a Chicago school—a rewarding job, which, the author says, "provides a captive audience on whom I test my children's stories." Married and the father of three children, Dennis Fradin spends his free time with his family or playing a myriad of sports and games with his childhood chums.

About the Artists:

Len Meents studied painting and drawing at Southern Illinois University and after graduation in 1969 he moved to Chicago. Mr. Meents works full time as a painter and illustrator. He and his wife and child currently make their home in LaGrange, Illinois.

Richard Wahl, graduate of the Art Center College of Design in Los Angeles, has illustrated a number of magazine articles and booklets. He is a skilled artist and photographer who advocates realistic interpretations of his subjects. He lives with his wife and two sons in Libertyville, Illinois.